Summary:

Never Split the Difference

By: Chris Voss

Proudly Brought to you by:

Legal & Disclaimer

Table of Contents

The Book at a Glance

This book is structured much like constructing a building. Each chapter is built upon the principles of the previous one. Some of the things you will learn are the techniques for *Active Listening*, haggling, and introduction of the *Black Swan* concept.

Chapter 2 will help you avoid incorrect assumptions of some negotiators and replace them with *Active Listening* techniques. You will also learn in this chapter how to buy more time and to really intuit your counterpart in order for them to feel understood and finally open up.

Tactical Empathy is the main lesson of Chapter 3. You will also learn the concept of *Accusation Audit* - disarming the complaints of your counterpart by speaking them aloud.

In Chapter 4, you will learn how to create an atmosphere of unconditional positive regard by affirming your counterpart. You will discover how to achieve this by using *Summaries* and *Paraphrasing*.

The principle of Chapter 5 is that "No" is what starts the negotiation. You will be taught the importance of negotiating in your counterpart's world and acknowledging their right to choose. Additionally, you will learn an email technique for you not to be rejected again.

The focus of Chapter 6 is the art of bending reality - setting up a negotiation in such a way that your counterpart will accept the rules you set for the discussion unconsciously.

Chapter 7 is all about the technique of *Calibrated Questions*. These are questions that begin with "How" or "What" instead of using "Yes or No" questions.

How to apply this concept will be demonstrated on Chapter 8, along with the importance of always using "Yes" with "How?", nonverbal communication, using "How" when saying "No", and others.

Chapter 9 introduces the *Ackerman System* - the most effective process the FBI use for setting up offers.

The *Black Swan,* which is the rarest negotiation tactic, will be discussed in depth in Chapter 10. The goal of this method is to uncover 3 to 5 game-changer information present in every negotiation.

Every chapter begins with a hostage negotiation story, which will be evaluated to find out what worked and what didn't. After presenting the theory, real-life examples will be shown to demonstrate how the techniques were actually applied.

FREE BONUSES

P.S. Is it okay if we overdeliver?

Here at Readtrepreneur Publishing, we believe in overdelivering way beyond our reader's expectations. Is it okay if we overdeliver?

Here's the deal, we're going to give you an extremely condensed PDF summary of the book which you've just read and much more...

What's the catch? We need to trust you... You see, we want to overdeliver and in order for us to do that, we've to trust our reader to keep this bonus a secret to themselves? Why? Because we don't want people to be getting our exclusive PDF summaries even without buying our books itself. Unethical, right?

Ok. Are you ready?

Firstly, remember that your book is code: "**READ61**".

Next, visit this link: **http://bit.ly/exclusivepdfs**

Everything else will be self explanatory after you've visited: **http://bit.ly/exclusivepdfs.**

We hope you'll enjoy our free bonuses as much as we enjoyed preparing it for you!

Chapter 1 The New Rules

How to Become the Smartest Person in Any Room

The most effective approach for negotiation is not by using formal academic methods. Proven and practical strategies derive from experience.

The lessons in this book can prove to be a great tool for more profitable relationships and interactions with other people.

We are all animals, or at least generally behave like one. This means that we make decisions driven by subtle fears, needs, desires, and beliefs. It is crucial that we understand and accept this reality in order to be able to have successful negotiations.

Almost all hostage scenarios are not rational problem solving situations.

In the real world, negotiation is not a robotic activity. It is far more complex than it seems. This requires us to dispose the mechanical approach and rather embrace the informal, but proven negotiation principles drawn from experience.

What we need are simple, easy to learn and apply psychological tactics to pacify emotions, develop rapport, earn trust, have the other party verbalize their needs, and convince the other party that we really understand them.

The foundation for an effective negotiation is the universal truth that people want empathy and acceptance. Listening and understanding is the most effective way to achieve this.

As shown in a psychotherapy research, people tend to listen to themselves and be clearer about their own thoughts and intentions when they feel they are really heard. Furthermore, knowing that they are well understood makes them less defensive and more logical.

This concept is known as *Tactical Empathy*. This is listening as a martial art, which aims to access the other person's mind by balancing emotional intelligence and influence. Listening does not mean being passive. It is the most active thing you can do for a successful negotiation.

Fortunately, not everyone has to be forced to negotiate with kidnappers for their loved one's life. However, *life is a negotiation.* This book is relevant not just for life-and-death situations, such as a hostage crisis, but also for things as simple as convincing your child to sleep early or buying an item at a lower price.

There are some steps to master negotiation in your daily life. The first one is to not be repugnant to negotiating. Embrace the fact that negotiation is an essential part of our life. We get what we ask for, but we have to ask properly.

The majority of our actions is driven by wants. Our ability to negotiate plays a crucial role in almost all aspect of our lives. It is crucial for you to get what you want without causing emotional damage to the other person. In other words, having a successful negotiation in a relationship-affirming way.

The principles presented in this book are designed to be effective in the real world. Preparation is critical for a successful negotiation. Negotiation is the heart of collaboration. It can make conflicts meaningful and profitable for both sides.

Chapter 2 Be A Mirror

A good negotiator prepares for possible surprises. A great one, on the other hand, uses skills to uncover the surprises that he is sure are lurking somewhere.

A lot of negotiators fail plainly because they do not question their current assumptions. Their minds are closed to new possibilities. This may be due to pride. Hence, they are unprepared for the unpredictable and complicated nature of real-life negotiations.

You have to approach the negotiation with a mindset of discovery. Aim to deduce as many information as you can.

All of us have natural biases. We usually have them because of our tendency to favor consistency rather than truth. This limits us to only listen selectively. In other words, we hear only that which we want to hear based on our biases.

Do not be overwhelmed with your own arguments. Focus instead on the other person and what they have to say.

Your goal is to get your counterpart to feel safe enough to open up in order for you to find out what they really need.

The key is active listening; really empathizing with your counterpart to the point that they know they can safely trust you.

It is also crucial to learn the skill of slowing things down. Be a people mover rather than a problem solver. This will help you to slow down the process. Slowing down the negotiation also calms down the situation. Besides, rushing the process may destroy the rapport you are trying to build with your counterpart.

Another great tool to use is the *Late-night FM DJ Voice*. This voice is characterized as tranquil and affirming.

Do not focus merely on the words you have to say. Also pay a great deal of attention to the way you deliver them. This is because our brain processes the feelings and intentions of people by their way of delivery as much as it does to plain words and actions. Your voice alone is a game-changer. It can instantly click an emotional switch even from bad to good.

Essentially, there are three different voice tones that negotiators can use: the late night FM DJ voice, the positive voice, and the assertive voice.

The FM DJ voice requires that you inflect your voice down. This will give an impression that you have it under control. On the contrary, having a rising intonation elicits response. This allows your counterpart to take the lead.

Your default voice should be playful or positive. This portrays a good-natured, light, and encouraging person. The key is to relax and smile while talking, even if it is just over the phone.

Take note that most people can think quicker and tend to collaborate more when they are in a positive state of mind.

The direct or assertive voice is used rarely. It usually hampers the process of building trust with your counterpart.

A bulk of this chapter is dedicated into the concept of *mirroring*. Also known as *isopraxism,* this tactic is built upon the biological principle that "we fear what is different and are attracted to what is similar". Its aim is to initiate bonding and build rapport between you and your counterpart.

Mirroring is done by repeating the last three words or at least the most critical word from the last statement of the one you are negotiating with. This will help further with the rapport building. Take note: the key to have a successful negotiation is not about being right, but about having the right mindset.

Mirroring enables you to disagree without being disagreeable – a skill crucial for a profitable negotiation. It serves a double purpose: having the clarity that you want and communicating respect and concern over what the other person is saying.

Here are the four steps to confront without having a confrontation:

1. Speak using the FM DJ voice.
2. Start with "I'm sorry…"
3. Mirror.
4. Silence. Give at least four seconds of silence to let the mirror work its magic on your counterpart.
5. Repeat.

The skill of mirroring takes practice in order for you to successfully apply it. However, mastering it pays a great dividend in all your social interactions and relationships.

Chapter 3 Don't Feel Their Pain, Label It

Emotions are the means to have a successful negotiation. This is so because the problems of your counterpart are their emotions. This requires that you focus on listening more than speaking.

The greater is your knowledge of someone, the greater will be your influence to them.

In any negotiation process, understanding the other party's side – tactical empathy - is vital. The opposite will only build up frustration and will make them more hesitant to agree with you. Tactical empathy does not mean compromising your values. It does not ask you to just agree with your counterpart's position.

Empathy is the ability to recognize and vocalize your counterpart's perspective. Its end goal is to increase your influence by "being influenced". This conveys to your counterpart that you are listening.

10

In doing this, you may have to deal with the negative emotions of your counterpart first as they can be more powerful than the reason they will make with the deal. The key is to drop off your personal agendas and focus on your counterpart's. You can be more authentic and effective in handling the situation when your focus is on the other party.

Your brain aligns with your counterpart's through a process called *neural resonance*. This is achieved by closely observing the other person's body language and tone of voice. However, a fMRI experiment revealed that neural resonance disappears when people communicate poorly.

The act of *labeling* involves identifying and verbalizing the emotions of your counterpart. This helps pacify their emotions, as they feel validated. Labeling their emotions communicates that you identify with how they really feel.

This tactic is especially useful in tense situations. This diffuses your counterpart's covert emotions as they are exposed.

The first step in applying the principle of labeling in your negotiations is by identifying your counterpart's emotional state. To do this, you have to closely observe their responses to external stimuli. Usually, you can create those stimuli by your words.

These usually begin with:

It seems like . . .

It sounds like . . .

It looks like . . .

Notice that the first person point-of-view is not used. The word "I" makes people more defensive. Using a neutral language encourages your counterpart to be more responsive. It nudges the other person to elaborate on his answers rather than just a plain "Yes" or "No".

The last step is silence. Silence will allow the effect of labeling to sink in.

When used properly, labeling is effective for neutralizing the negative and reinforcing the positive dynamics of the negotiation. This is simply because of the fact that

12

all human beings have a need to be appreciated and understood.

There are two levels of people's emotions: the "presenting" behavior and the "underlying" feelings. The presenting behavior is the one that we can readily sense by seeing and hearing. However, what drives the behavior is the "underlying" emotion.

Good negotiators address those underlying emotions. Labeling diffuses the negatives or reinforces the positives. This tactic is effective when you are making an apology.

Research has proven that the best way to handle negativity is by observing it without reacting or judging. Afterwards, replace those negative emotions with positive ones.

Labeling fear interrupts the amygdala, the part of the brain that reacts to threats, clearing the obstacles to generate more positive emotions.

Empathy is a potent mood enhancer. However, this is not always easy. Sometimes you need to peel layer by layer of negative emotions in order to achieve the desired result.

Another powerful tactic is to use an *accusation audit*. An accusation audit is listing every negative thing your opponent may throw at you during the negotiation. Tackling negativity right on brings you to the zone of empathy. Speaking those negativities aloud may nudge the other person to claim that quite the opposite is true.

Each skill in this book is presented as if they were musical instruments. In real life, however, the band must play simultaneously. Hence, you must learn how to conduct.

Think of these negotiation tactics as a natural part of a natural healthy human interaction rather than artificial conversation tic. They will seem inauthentic at first. As you keep on practicing them, they will help create more meaningful relationships. Take note: The primary aim is human connection. Achieving what you desire is only a bonus.

Chapter 4 Beware "Yes" – Master "No"

One of society's biggest dictums is "Be nice". The principle presented in this chapter goes directly against this. Hence, many will find this difficult to apply.

It is interesting to note, however, that niceties are often times ruse. This is fatal for negotiators, as their aim is to understand the wants and needs of their counterpart and extract as much information as possible.

Hence, aiming for your counterpart's "No" rather than their typical "Yes" is extremely powerful. In this way, you will determine their boundaries and discover their wants based on their "No".

Think of this principle as anti – "niceness ruse". Achieving your counterpart's "No" peels away inauthenticity that is a hamper for a successful negotiation.

Break the habit of forcing people to say "Yes" as it can turn people angry and defensive. This will blind them to see reality.

Contrary to popular belief, receiving "No" as an answer is not a failure. It usually just means "Wait" or "I'm not comfortable". It is not the end of the negotiation. It is only the beginning.

Of course, "Yes" is the ultimate goal in any negotiation. However, don't strive for it early on.

The need for safety and control is one of our basic needs. Being able to say "No" helps your counterpart to obtain that, calming their emotions, and creating a more constructive and collaborative environment.

This calls for you to train yourself to get used to hearing "No". Do not take them personally and literally. Don't just expect your counterpart to say "No". Get them to say it early on.

There are three different kinds of "Yes". They are the Counterfeit, Confirmation, and Commitment.

A counterfeit "yes" is usually said by a person who does not really want to make the deal, but somehow feels that saying "Yes" is the only way to escape the conversation. It could also be that your counterpart just wants to keep the conversation in order to obtain more information.

A confirmation "yes" is often just a result of a salesperson pushing you. However, this is not usually backed up with action.

What you really want is the commitment "yes". This one is authentic and leads to the action you desire.

Using your skills to build rapport and get the deal with the other person is useful only to the extent that they also feel they are at least equally responsible.

Yes, we can never control other people's decision. Nevertheless, we can influence them by seeing things according to their worldview.

Being nice alone in a negotiation is manipulative and inauthentic. These are usually the characteristics of an early "yes".

On the other hand, "No" enables you to tackle the real issue head on. It keeps people from making ineffective decisions. A "No" slow things down, helping people embrace the deals that they are getting into. Ultimately, "No" moves everyone forward.

Don't just aim to be able to accept your counterpart's "No". Go one step further by intentionally getting it. In fact, there are times that the only way you can have the other party engage with you is by forcing them into a "No".

One way to do this is by mislabeling your counterpart's emotions or wants. This forces them to say "No".

A more straightforward approach is to ask the other party what they don't want. Be careful, however, with persons whom you can't get to say "No". They are either confused, undecided, or with a hidden agenda.

In other words, no "no" means no go.

Winning in a negotiation is not about how smart you are. It is about convincing your counterpart that you have the same goal as them. Remember: it's not about you.

Chapter 5 Triggering The Two Words That Immediately Transform Any Negotiation

As explained in the previous chapter, the common niceties of "yeses" and "you're rights" are not a substitute for having authentic conversations and building profitable relationships.

Only when you convinced a person that you truly understood his perception and worldview can you influence him into some emotional and behavioral changes.

In psychology, there is a concept called *unconditional positive regard*, which is popularized by the great American psychologist Carl Rogers. Carl Rogers proposed that an authentic change will only occur when a therapist embraces the client despite who they are - accepting them unconditionally.

From our childhood, we were conditioned to think that we are accepted or not on the basis of our behaviors.

This develops in us a tendency to hide our real self in order to be approved by others.

This approach works because the more a person feels understood, the more they are encouraged to behave constructively.

Another great tool is to use *summary* to have your counterpart say "That's right". This will also convey that you are really getting their point. Notice, it is "That's right" and not "You're right".

Receiving "You're right" is usually a disaster. Your counterpart may agree with you theoretically without really taking responsibility for the conclusion. "You're right" is also sometimes used to get the other person to quit on bothering you.

Using "That's right" is also extremely useful for you in making sales, for corporate career success, and any other aspects of life.

"That's right" is the foundation of a good summary and paraphrasing, both of which affirm the other person.

Chapter 6 Bend Their Reality

Contrary to popular belief, negotiation is not a linear process. This is because we are somehow irrational and driven by hidden urges.

By acknowledging and understanding this reality, you can be able to bend your counterpart's reality to conform to what you really want.

It is highly important to not compromise your ground in the negotiation. Many negotiation experts impose the win-win mindset. However, this is usually not effective and can lead to disaster. It fails to satisfy both parties at its best.

To compromise – split the difference – is usually a bad deal. You can think of it this way: A lady wants her man to wear black shoes paired with his suit. However, he prefers to wear brown shoes. Hence, they both agreed to compromise and meet halfway: the husband wears a black shoe on one foot and a brown shoe on the other.

Isn't wearing either complete black shoes or brown shoes way better?

The problem is that compromise is known to be a great concept in many aspects of life. The thing is that compromise seems easier and safer for us. Almost all negotiators are driven by fear or by the avoidance of pain. Only few are driven by their goals. Here's the rule: don't ever split the difference.

Time is one of the most vital factors in negotiations. Therefore, it is crucial to understand how deadlines affect us and the outcome of the conversation.

A deadline can trick you into believing that making a deal now with a compromise is better than having a good deal. Be careful to avoid making an impulsive decision, especially when faced with a deadline. We tend to rush as the deadline approaches. Good negotiators resist this urge and take advantage of it on their counterpart.

Besides, deadlines are usually arbitrary and flexible. They usually do not inflict the consequence that we think it will. Therefore, there is no need to be anxious and rattled.

It is better to not have a deal than to have a bad one. Take note that the negotiation is also over for the other side when it is over for one party.

Hiding your deadline puts you in the worst possible condition. It significantly increases the likelihood of being in an impasse. Having a personal deadline and hiding it forces you to concede quickly, while your counterpart thinks that they have more time. To hide your deadline is to negotiate with self. This always leads to defeat.

Deadlines are usually never fixed. The point is to have a feel for how long the negotiation will be.

In a negotiation, there is actually no such thing as fair. You are wrong to think that your counterpart thinks like you in the negotiation. Thinking that way is projection, not empathy.

The truth is that we are all somehow irrational and emotional beings. Emotion plays a vital role in making decisions. We can logically reason to arrive at a decision, but emotion governs how we decide.

The F–word – "fair" – is the most powerful word in any negotiation. Human beings are naturally driven by how much we feel respected. People agree when they know they are fairly treated and protest if they don't.

Brain-imaging studies have shown that the insular cortex – the part of the brain that regulates emotions – reflects the degree of unfairness in our interactions. This is true even in nonhuman primates.

The negative emotion of unfairness outweighs the rational positive value of having something.

Being aware that the word "fairness" is much more complicated than it seems to be, you need to use it very carefully. Remember that your reputation precedes you. Hence, aim for a reputation of being fair.

A way to bend other people's reality is to determine the underlying motives why they buy. For example, what a good babysitter really sells is not childcare, but a relaxed evening. A furnace salesperson delivers cozy rooms for family time, and a locksmith provides a sense of security.

Not because our decisions are largely irrational does it mean that there are no patterns and principles explaining how we act. Psychologists Daniel Kahneman and Amos Tversky created a theory in 1971 that best explains the principles of our irrational behaviors. This is called the *Prospect Theory*.

It states that people are drawn to certainty over risk even when the latter is a better choice. This is also known as the *Certainty Effect*. Furthermore, the principle of *Loss Aversion* argues that people tend to take greater risks avoiding losses than achieving gains.

In order to have some leverage, you have to convince the other party that they have something massive to lose if they do not get the deal.

Chapter 7 Create The Illusion Of Control

Negotiation is coaxing, not overcoming. It is about co-opting and not defeating. Most importantly, a successful negotiation means having your counterpart not just do the work for you, but also be able to suggest your solution himself.

A great tool to achieve this is called the *calibrated*, or *open-ended question*. These questions remove aggression by addressing the other party's side openly and without resistance. This allows you to nudge them by being able to present ideas and offers without being pushy.

Avoid verbal flexing – talking with your counterpart merely to force them to see things your way. This aggravates tension and breaks down the negotiation.

A negotiation done well is an information-gathering process that nudges your counterpart in favor of you.

You can gradually have them adopt your point of view by working to getting the other side drop their unbelief. They key is to not directly convince them of your own ideas. Rather, you ride them to your ideas.

In fact, half of your job as a negotiator is to stop your opponent's unbelieving. One of the most powerful ways to achieve this is by asking calibrated questions. This gives them the illusion of control.

There is, however, a very important condition to consider: how those calibrated questions are delivered. The effect of those questions upon your counterpart largely depends on the tone and the overall emotion of your voice.

Be careful not to make it sound like an accusation or threat. By speaking calmly, the other person will take it as a problem to be solved and not as an insult.

What makes those calibrated questions work is that they are not explicit, leaving it open for your counterpart's interpretation. Contrary to statements, they have no subject of attack. More so, they are designed to enlighten your counterpart about the problem rather than directly telling what the problem is.

You give them direction by first figuring out where you want the conversation to be and designing queries that will propel the conversation to go there, while the other person still thinks they are the one gaining the upper hand.

Calibrating those questions has a clear format to be followed. Here are those:

Calibrated questions do not use verbs like *can, do, does, is,* and *are*. This is because these types of questions are answerable by "Yes" or "No", thus making them too rigid.

Rather, use what people known as reporters', or W-H questions. Those are *what, where, when, why, who, and how.* This will encourage the other person to really analyze the situation and speak more expansively.

However, it is even better to begin with "what" and "how", or occasionally "why", rather than "what", "where", and "when". The latter questions will just cause the other person to give information without thinking. Whereas "why" can boomerang. "Why" must only be used if the defensiveness caused supports the change you aim to have.

Calibrated questions should be used early and often.

The implication of a well-designed calibrated question is that you have the same wants with your counterpart, but you need their intelligence to obtain it.

You can calibrate almost any question to make them less harsh and accusatory. The secret to getting your counterpart adopt your perspective is not by confronting their ideas right on, but by acknowledging them openly. This makes your opponent feel like they're in charge, but you know that just the opposite is true.

In employing this tactic, take note that having self-control is pivotal. How can you expect to control the emotion of the other party if you can't lead your own feelings? Learning how to use the best skills is useless if you cannot regulate yourself.

The primary rule in order to keep in control of your emotion is by biting your tongue – avoid knee-jerk, impulsive reactions.

Another thing is to not counterattack when verbally assaulted. The point is that when people feel they are not in control, they adopt a *hostage mentality*.

You have to train your neocortex – the part of your brain which rationalizes – to override the reactive parts of the brain.

Chapter 8 Guarantee Execution

"Yes" is useless without "How". An agreement is good. However, a contract is better and a signed check is best.

This is the importance of "How" questions. This type of question pressures the other person to come up with answers and analyze your problems.

It is possible to read and set the negotiation environment in favor of your goals by using these "How" questions. You have to have an idea where you want the conversation to go while making your questions.

The trick here is that "How" questions are indirect and a graceful way to say "No", provided that they are rightly delivered. They encourage the other person to devise a better solution, your solution, to solve the problem. "How" questions gently delivered invites collaboration and makes your counterpart feel respected.

It is very important to be aware of the tone of your voice, because it is just as critical as the question itself. This phrase can be communicated as an accusation or a request for assistance.

Using "How" questions influences others to take a positive look at the problem at hand. This is called "forced empathy".

Aside from being able to say "No" covertly and politely, the other key importance of asking "How?" is that it pushes your counterpart to consider and elaborate how a deal they offered will be implemented. Poor implementation leads to poor profits.

Having your counterpart articulate how a deal will be done using their own words will give them the impression that the solution is their own idea. People tend to be more dedicated in implementing an idea that they think they have come up with. This is the reason negotiation is often defined as "the art of letting someone else have your way".

Here are the two key questions you can use to make your counterpart think that they are defining success in their own terms: "How will we know we're on track?" and "How will we address things if we find we're off track?" Summarize their answer to these until you obtain their "That's right". This is how you can say they've bought in.

Remember to be aware of the two signs indicating that your counterpart doesn't believe the idea is theirs. One is what was discussed previously: when they say "You're right".

The other one is when they say "I'll try" as a response to you pushing an implementation. This phrase basically means "I plan to fail".

When you get these responses, proceed by asking more calibrated "How" questions until they articulated the terms of a successful deal using their own voice. Lastly, summarize their statement until you get a "That's right".

Let your opponent feel victory. Give them the illusion that the idea was theirs. Do not let your ego take control.

In every negotiation, you have to take consideration not just the one whom you are talking to, but the entire negotiation space. Take note: it only takes one person to ruin the deal. You can avoid a disastrous negotiation by doing this.

Effective negotiators are aware not just of verbal, but also the para verbal (how words are said) and nonverbal aspect of the communication. They know how to use these for their benefit. Changing even just a word can greatly influence your counterpart's decision.

A repetitive string of "What" and "How" questions can help you avert the manipulation of an opponent.

UCLA psychology professor Albert Mehrabian created the 7-38-55 rule in his famous studies of what makes us like or dislike a person. This rule states that the communication actually consists of only 7 percent of words, 38 percent from the tone of your voice, and 55 percent from your face and body language. In other words, your general body language and vocal tone are actually more powerful than your words.

You can utilize this principle to have a successful negotiation. First, observe closely if the vocal tone and body language of your counterpart aligns with their words. If they don't, it could be an indication that they are not telling the truth.

This will help ensure that the agreement will be followed through by your counterpart. Furthermore, this act of gently checking incongruence by labeling will make the other person feel respected.

There is a great tool you can use to avoid the trap of having your counterpart give a counterfeit "yes". This is called the *Rule of Three*. This is simply getting the other person to agree to the same thing three times in a conversation.

Be careful, however, as there is a risk of seeming too pushy when you use this tactic. The way to avoid this is to vary your tactics. You can employ the different tactics discussed in this book.

For example, deem the first "yes" of your counterpart as a "no". You can do labeling or summary on the second time so that they will say "That's right". Then you can use a calibrated "What" or "How" question on the third time.

You may also try to deliver the same question in three different ways.

Try this the next time you doubt your counterpart's truthfulness or authenticity.

Another concept you can utilize is the *Pinocchio Effect*. This simply explains that the number of words grow in direct proportion to the number of lies. People who are lying tend to be defensive because they worry about being believed.

Pay attention to the number of personal pronouns the other person is using. The more they use personal pronouns, such as "I", "my", and "me", the less prominent they actually are. The converse of this is also true. This is so because smart negotiators tend to defer from the people in order for them not to be cornered into making a decision.

Using your name is a great way to create "forced empathy". It enables your counterpart to see you more as a person. Humanize yourself by using your name while introducing self. Deliver it in a fun and friendly manner.

You can opt to push your counterparts to bid against themselves. The best way to do this is by getting your counterparts to say "no" by asking "how" questions.

Usually, there are four ways of saying "No" before actually mentioning the exact word. The first step is to deliver "How am I supposed to do that?" in a deferential manner. Next is some version of "Your offer is very generous, I'm sorry, that just doesn't work for me". This one helps you avoid counteroffers and build empathy.

Then you can ask something like, "I'm sorry but I'm afraid I just can't do that". This one is more direct. The phrase "can't do that" can trigger your counterpart's empathy towards you, as it is an expression of your lack of ability.

A bit more succinct version is "I'm sorry, no". Delivered properly, this will not seem to be negative at all.

Simply saying the word "No" is obviously the most direct one. Be careful to deliver it with a downward inflection and in a pleasant tone.

Be very careful with the way you say "no". Maintain your focus and discipline until the very end. There are certain points, especially at the finale, when your mental discipline becomes more critical. Don't allow your mind to wander.

Chapter 9 Bargain Hard

The part of negotiation that causes the most anxiety and aggression is bargaining. Hence, this is the part that is most commonly mishandled.

Skilled bargainers see the psychological urges that are driving the whole process.

WHAT TYPE ARE YOU?

Your negotiating style is developed by your childhood, family, schooling, culture, and a lot of other factors. By discovering it, you can find out what yours and your counterpart's negotiating strengths and weaknesses are. This will help you formulate a more effective mindset and strategy.

Negotiation style is a crucial factor in bargaining. Knowing what instinctively drives your decision in different circumstances will give you the right approach in gaming out some tactics.

Here are the three broad types of negotiators:

- **Analysts**

Analysts are diligent and methodical. They do not tend to rush. Their principle is that time is of little consequence as they aim to work toward the best solution in a systematic way. Their self-image is based on reducing errors.

A typical Analyst prefers to work on his own. They don't show emotion most of the time and usually employ the *late-night FM DJ voice*.

However, they often speak in a cold and distant way. Analysts are proud of not missing any detail because of their extensive preparation. They hate surprises. They will research for weeks to get information that they might obtain in a few minutes at the negotiation table.

Analysts are reserved negotiators. They are also extremely sensitive to reciprocity. If they don't get something in return upon giving their own within a certain time period, they will easily disengage. They are skeptical by nature.

40

They are not going to answer you until they fully understand what will be the results of doing so. Hence, asking so many questions to start with is not a good idea.

In dealing with them, focus on the facts. Use clear data to direct your reason. Warn them of risks early on to avoid surprises.

For them, silence is an opportunity to think. Don't interpret it as they are mad at you or allowing you to talk more. Have them talk first if you feel they are not seeing things according to your perspective.

Apologies do not matter that much to them. This is because they view their relationship with you and the negotiation itself as separate things. They are not quick to respond to questions, especially when the answer is "Yes".

If you fall into this category, be careful not to disconnect from an essential source of data – your counterpart. The biggest thing you can do is to smile while you speak.

41

- **Accommodator**

The most important thing for Accommodators is building relationship with their counterpart. They aim to be on great terms with the other party. Hence, they prefer win-win solutions.

Accommodators are great at building rapport. However, this does not necessarily mean that they are moving forward in the negotiation. They want to be friends with their counterpart even without reaching an agreement. They are optimistic and peace-seeking.

However, they are also distractible and poor time managers. For an Accommodator, time is equivalent to relationship.

- **Assertive**

The Assertive negotiators believe time is money. They judge themselves based on how much they accomplish in a time period. They are very competitive, sometimes overly. They view business relationships solely based on respect. Most of all, they want to be heard. They are not able to listen to you unless they feel heard by you first.

One downside with them, however, is that they focus more on their goals than on people. They tell more than they were asked of.

This means that the best approach in dealing with Assertive types is to convince them that you really understand them. This is the only way for them to open up to your point of view.

Every silence is a chance to speak more to an Assertive. The most important thing is to have them say "That's right".

Assertive negotiators have the "give an inch/take a mile" mindset. They tend to think they deserve whatever you give them, making them oblivious to expectations of paying you back.

If you belong to this type, be aware of your tone. You will often sound overly harsh even when you don't actually intend to be so. Intentionally work out on improving your tone – making it more pleasant. Employ calibration and labels to be friendlier.

Assertive negotiators will interpret your silence as either you simply have nothing to say or you want them to talk.

The greatest hindrance to identifying your counterpart's negotiation style negatively is the "I am normal" paradox. This is the assumption that others see the world the same way we see it. This is among the most damaging mentality in any negotiation. Having this mindset unconsciously projects your own style with that of the other.

The three types differ in their way of preparation even in the way they approach the conversation. Before anything else, you have to identify the other person's "normal".

The Black Swan rule states that you have to treat others the way they need, not just *want*, to be treated.

TAKING A PUNCH

Negotiation academics treat the negotiation process as something rational and void of emotions. Nothing could be further from the truth.

44

In real life, experienced negotiators usually set an extreme anchor – a ridiculous offer. Because your aim is to gather information, you will want to have the other guy set an offer first. Welcome the extreme anchor.

However, extreme anchoring is powerful with the fact that you are human. Your emotions may arise. When this happens, proceed to take the punch without responding angrily or bidding against self.

The first thing to do is to deflect the attack in a manner that opens up your opponent. Say "No" in ways already discussed or ask calibrated questions. You can also pivot to terms or shift the focus to nonmonetary terms. Responding this way refocus the other person when you feel you are prone to compromise.

If the other side forces you to make the first offer, cite an extremely high price someone else might charge. Your aim is to suck information from your counterpart.

PUNCHING BACK: USING ASSERTION WITHOUT GETTING USED BY IT

Hit the other person hard when the negotiation seems to be slow towards a resolution. This will shake them out of a narrow mentality.

This is a real challenge if you are not naturally assertive. Here are the effective ways to do this smartly:

- **REAL ANGER, THREATS WITHOUT ANGER, AND STRATEGIC UMBRAGE**

A research conducted by Marwan Sinaceur of INSEAD and Larissa Tiedens of Stanford University found that angry expressions increase a negotiator's edge and final take. Anger implies passion and conviction that can influence your counterpart to concede. However, your counterpart's cognitive ability lessens as their sensitivity to threats is increased. This may lead to bad concessions and implementation problems, ultimately limiting your take.

Take note: researchers also found that expressions of inauthentic anger backfire. This destroys trust, causing balky demands. Anger must be real in order to be effective. Be sure to control it, as it also reduces your ability to think clearly.

When someone gives you a ridiculous offer, take a deep breath and channel a little anger at the proposal, then say, "I don't see how that would ever work". This well-timed receiving of offense is what we call the "strategic umbrage". This can awaken your counterpart to the issue.

Daniel Ames and Abbie Wazlawek of Columbia University found that people on the receiving end of the umbrage were more likely to consider themselves as *overassertive*, even when the other side didn't think so. The main point here is to be conscious how this might be used against you.

Delivering threats devoid of anger but with confidence and control is a great tactic.

- **"WHY QUESTIONS"**

  As discussed earlier, "Why?" makes people defensive. Nonetheless, there is a way to ask "Why?" effectively – use the defensiveness induced by the question to have your counterpart defend your stance. In other words, if you want to draw a counterpart to your side, ask, "Why would you do that?", given that "that" is on your favor.

For example, if you aim to pull a customer away from the competitor, you can say, "Why would you ever do business with me? Why would you ever change from your current supplier? They're great!" This type of questions nudges your counterpart to work in service of you.

- **"I" MESSAGES**

  This is a great way to set a limit without inducing confrontation. The word "I" in a question strategically shifts your counterpart's focus onto you enabling them to get your point.

  The traditional use of "I" is to press the pause button and get out of a bad dynamic. Make sure that you use "I" not in an aggressive or argumentative manner.

- **NO NEEDINESS: HAVING THE READY-TO-WALK MINDSET**

Never be desperate for a deal. If you are not able to say "No", you've got yourself a hostage.

Be reminded of the massive importance of maintaining a collaborative relationship with your counterpart. Respond in a manner of *tough love* – strong and clear but empathic – not of violence or hatred.

Use strong emotions such as anger minimally, and never as a personal attack. In any negotiation, never look at your counterpart as an enemy. The other person is never the problem. Rather, they are the unsettled issue. Focus on it.

A last resort is pushing back. Your counterpart will no longer feel imprisoned in a negative situation when they have a chance to step back and breathe. They will appreciate you for giving them back a sense of autonomy. Refrain from creating an enemy.

ACKERMAN BARGAINING

The Ackerman Bargaining is a model of haggling employing the offer-counteroffer method. This is named after Mike Ackerman, a former CIA member, who is the founder of a kidnap-for-ransom company.

The Ackerman method consists of these steps:

1. **Set the price you are aiming for.**
2. **Set your initial offer at 65 percent of your original price.**

The shocking effect of this extreme anchor will arouse the primal "fight-or-flight" reaction in almost all negotiators. This will exhaust your counterpart's cognitive resources, forcing them to make a rash decision.

3. **Compute three levels of decrease (to 85, 95, and 100 percent).**

   This act encourages your counterpart to also concede. Your counterpart is more likely to make concessions to those who take the initiative to compromise. This is explained by the rule of reciprocity.

Also, this gives your counterpart the illusion of squeezing you into absolute exhaustion. This effectively boosts their self-esteem. Research has shown that people tend to feel better about the negotiation process when they are getting concessions than when they are offered a single fixed "fair" offer.

4. **Employ much empathy and various ways of saying "No" to get the other side to counter before you increase your offer.**

5. **Use non-round numbers when calculating the final amount.**

   As already explained earlier, this gives it weight and credibility.

6. **Finally, offer a nonmonetary term.**

   This is to imply that you have really reached your limit.

This system incorporates all the tactics discussed here without you consciously thinking of each of them.

Chapter 10 Finding the Black Swan

FINDING LEVERAGE IN THE PREDICTABLY UNPREDICTABLE

The concept of Black Swan was made popular by Nassim Nicholas Taleb in his bestselling books *Fooled by Randomness* and *The Black Swan*. However, the term was already coined long before.

It never occurred to people - not until the seventeenth century - that black swans also exist. It was the Dutch explorer Willem de Vlamingh who first discovered one in 1697 at Western Australia. Since then, "Black Swans" became a common metaphor people use for impossible things in the seventeenth century London.

Taleb used the term to refer to the vanity of predictions based on previous experience. The Black Swans are pieces of information outside our common expectations, hence unpredictable.

In all negotiations, there are three types of information: the *known knowns, known unknowns, and the unknown unknowns.* The *known knowns* are the things that we already know. The *known unknowns* are those we are sure that exist but is unknown to us. However, the real game changers are those that we do not know that we don't know – the Black Swans.

UNCOVERING UNKNOWN UNKNOWNS

Firmly holding on to your expectations has a massive drawback – not valuing bits and pieces of information in the negotiation. Every case you handle is new.

You can be guided by what you know – your *known knowns.* However, never allow them to blind you. Have an open-mind in every situation. Be flexible and adaptable. Never overestimate your experiences and underestimate the information in front of you every moment of the negotiation process.

Finding a Black Swan and acting on it requires a mindset shift. It demands you to view the negotiation process in a multi-dimensional way.

Finding Black Swans is challenging because we are all, in one way or another, blind. There simply are things that we do not know that we don't know, and those things can ruin you or your deal.

A tip is that most people don't really know how to articulate the information they need unless they're carefully asked. The problem is that traditional research and interrogation techniques are designed to merely validate *known knowns* and minimize uncertainty. They don't go deeper into the unknowns.

It is those who are able to uncover and adopt to the unknowns that will be great. Ask many questions. Read your counterpart's nonverbal hints and always voice it out to them.

Don't aim to merely verify your expectations. Instead, open yourself to the current reality. Take note: negotiation is more comparable to walking on a tightrope than competing against an enemy. Focusing too much on the end goal will distract you from the next step. Concentrate rather on the next step until you finally arrive at your objective.

54

Your counterpart always has chunks of information whose value are unknown to them.

THE THREE TYPES OF LEVERAGE

One reason why Black Swans are useful is that they multiply leverage. They help you take over.

Theoretically, leverage means the ability to exact loss and withhold gain. In practice, however, the actual leverage that exists against you usually doesn't matter as much as the leverage the other side thinks you have on them. This is due to the reality of our irrational perceptions. Leverage is an emotional concept. Therefore, it can be made up whether it actually exists or not.

Among the many inputs of leverage are time, necessity, and competition. For instance, you have lesser leverage if you have to sell something before a given deadline than if you don't have a time constraint. Take note, however, that leverage and power are not the same.

You should always be aware of which side feels they will incur the most loss if the negotiation doesn't work out.

You have to convince the other party that not having the deal would be a real loss for them.

Here are the three kinds of leverage:

- **POSITIVE LEVERAGE**

    Positive leverage is your ability to give or withhold what your counterpart wants. In other words, you gain a positive leverage whenever the other person says, "I want (something)".

    In case you are trying to sell something, it would be better if you have contacts with the other buyers. You can use it to build an atmosphere of competition, forcing them to make a choice.

    You gain more power when your counterpart expresses their desire. This is the reason why experienced negotiators have their counterpart make the first offer – they want to keep their leverage.

- **NEGATIVE LEVERAGE**

    This type of leverage is what most people have in mind when they hear the word "leverage".

This is a negotiator's ability to make the other party to suffer using threats.

This effectively captures people's attention because of the concept of *loss aversion*. We are more driven to avoid loss than having similar gain.

Effective negotiators gather information that shows what matters most to their counterpart. Those are often not clearly revealed. The most effective way to achieve this is by interacting with your counterpart.

However, making threats, direct or subtle, is not recommended. They can be like bombs, inflicting a toxic residue that is hard to clean. You have to deal with the negative consequences carefully or else you might hurt yourself or ruin the whole process.

Furthermore, your counterpart can view your threats as your attempt to steal their autonomy. The problem is that people will usually prefer to die than lay down their autonomy. At best, they will simply close the negotiation irrationally.

57

A more covert tactic is to label your negative leverage. This makes the threat clear without assaulting.

- **NORMATIVE LEVERAGE**

  Normative leverage involves using your counterpart's beliefs and norms for your own gain. This is achieved by showing gaps between your opponent's ideals and actions.

  Listen to their language and speak accordingly with them.

KNOW THEIR RELIGION

You can truly influence your counterpart by understanding their worldview – the way they see things. Understanding them is a prerequisite in order for you to persuade them. In any negotiation, what leads to success is your ability to listen and not how well you speak.

In a hostage situation, among the primary things you have to find out is whether your counterparts see themselves living in their vision of future. You can use this information to formulate a negative leverage. Nevertheless, be careful about going all out with this

NEVER SPLIT THE DIFFERENCE

because of a phenomenon called the "paradox of power" - the harder you push, the stronger will be the resistance. Use negative leverage sparingly.

Seeking to understand your counterpart's worldview by listening can help you obtain a Black Swan that may shift the whole dynamics of the negotiation. Positioning your offers in accordance with your counterpart's worldview in making decisions have them feel respected. This gets their attention that gets you results.

Using your counterpart's religion is highly effective because it has major authority over them. Here are two tips for identifying your counterpart's religion accurately:

- Double-check everything you hear.
- Have backup listeners whose task is to listen between lines.

Listen, listen again, and listen some more.

THE SIMILARITY PRINCIPLE

This principle states that we trust those people whom we consider similar or familiar more than those who are not.

To belong is our primal instinct. Convincing the other person that you see things the same way they see them will instantly get you the influence.

THE POWER OF HOPES AND DREAMS

Having identified and truly understood your counterpart's worldview and aspirations in life, you can use these to have them follow you.

From childhood, all of us are dreaming of achieving something extraordinary in life. Unfortunately, along the way, as we grow older, people around us – our parents, teachers, friends, and others – bend our focus to what cannot be from what is possible. We begin to doubt.

This is why we tend to follow those who show an enthusiasm about our aspirations and deliver a clear plan on how we can achieve them.

Voice out your passion for them to achieve their goals. This will help you naturally lead them.

RELIGION AS A REASON

Studies have shown that people are more likely to positively respond to requests made in a good tone of voice and with a "because" reason.

You'll be more effective by giving reasons in accordance with your counterpart's religion.

IT'S NOT CRAZY, IT'S A CLUE

It is our nature to lash out or at least run away when faced with the unknown. Usually, it is labeled in negotiations using dismissing terms, such as, "They're crazy!"

However, the moment we're ready to give up and blurt, "They're crazy!" is usually the best moment to uncover Black Swans that will transform the dynamics of the negotiation.

In those moments of desperation, you have a choice: to push forward harder into the unknown or succumb to failure by simply concluding that the negotiation was useless.

61

GET FACE TIME

No amount of research will enable you to obtain some information that you want. There are those that can only be obtained when you go face-to-face with your counterpart.

It is very hard to extract Black Swans from your counterpart using emails because it gives them too much time to analyze the situation. This is the case even if you employ all the tactics discussed here very well. More so, email and other written communications limit your ability to decipher your counterpart, because nonverbal clues, such as the tone of voice and body language, are not visible.

OBSERVE UNGUARDED MOMENTS

Formal meetings, structured interactions, and planned negotiations often reveal the least Black Swan. Those are the moments when people are most aware and guarded. That's why it could be more profitable to hunt Black Swans on unstructured, spontaneous interactions.

WHEN IT DOESN'T MAKE SENSE, THERE'S CENTS TO BE MADE

Black Swans are anything outside your knowledge that changes things. Do not be deterred by confusing things. Rather, press harder forward and free your mind while searching for ways to get the most out of the negotiation.

Conclusion

The main purpose of this book is to move you from fear of conflict and enable to resolve conflicts with empathy. Most people naturally avoid conflict. They fear that things will lead to personal offenses that they cannot handle. This is especially true in close relationships.

If you are going to be great at any pursuit, you have to master the art of negotiation. Resist the urge to withdraw yourself or lash out. Embrace regular and well-thought conflict as the premise of profitable negotiations and of life.

In Chapter 1, the importance of not being constrained by rigid conventional insights about negotiation is emphasized. It is pointed out that almost all traditional academic approaches to negotiation are ineffective. This is because we are all somehow irrational. Our decisions are largely driven by our emotions. Unless we accept this fact, we cannot open our mind and adopt to the ever wavering circumstances in real life negotiations.

Chapter 2 reiterated the same concept in the previous chapter – current assumptions often blind negotiators. Instead, you should have an attitude of discovery. Tactics such as slowing down the negotiation to buy time, using the *late night FM DJ Voice*, and *mirroring* are also discussed here on details. These techniques are used to formulate a *four step process* to confront without confrontation.

Chapter 3 is largely dedicated to the principle of *labeling*. You have learned here that labeling is powerful because it neutralizes the negative and reinforces the positive dynamics of a negotiation.

You also learned how to use an *accusation audit* to help you deal with confrontations.

The conventional mindset that we should strive to get "Yes" and avoid "No" at all cost is shattered in Chapter 4. Here, you have learned that being able to say "no" gives your counterpart a sense of safety and autonomy –

primal needs of humans. Therefore, you must not only expect or embrace "no". You have to actually make an effort to extract it from the other person.

The two sweetest words in negotiations, "That's right", are explained here in detail. This makes the other person feel understood and respected. Hence, they will open up for a more collaborative discussion.

Chapter 6 gave you invaluable tips on bending to your counterpart's reality. These include the importance of not compromising your offer, using time for your advantage, and using the F-word - fair.

Chapter 7 equipped you to be able to give your opponent the illusion of control. This is achieved by using calibrated questions. The idea is that those calibrated questions will help you to nudge them towards a solution – your solution – to the problem by making them responsible. They will also think that your solution is their own idea.

The negotiation is never done without the actual implementation. This is the main lesson in Chapter 8.

"Yes" is useless without "How". How to use "How" questions effectively to guarantee execution is elaborated here. Some tips on influencing the other key players behind the negotiation table, spotting liars, and reading nonverbal clues are also the key points in this chapter.

Chapter 9 is dedicated to the tactic called *haggling*. The three major types of negotiators, how to use assertion, using "Why" questions, and the Ackerman Bargaining are among the key lessons here.

The Chapter 10 is all about the *Black Swan*. Black Swans are among those that we don't know that we don't know – *unknown unknowns*. Those pieces of information are the game changers in any negotiation.

This book gave you the most effective negotiating techniques you can employ to have a successful negotiation. They are now at your disposal. It is now up to you to use them to have more meaningful, authentic, and profitable relationships.

FREE BONUSES

P.S. Is it okay if we overdeliver?

Here at Readtrepreneur Publishing, we believe in overdelivering way beyond our reader's expectations. Is it okay if we overdeliver?

Here's the deal, we're going to give you an extremely condensed PDF summary of the book which you've just read and much more...

What's the catch? We need to trust you... You see, we want to overdeliver and in order for us to do that, we've to trust our reader to keep this bonus a secret to themselves? Why? Because we don't want people to be getting our exclusive PDF summaries even without buying our books itself. Unethical, right?

Ok. Are you ready?

Firstly, remember that your book is code: "**READ61**".

Next, visit this link: **http://bit.ly/exclusivepdfs**

Everything else will be self explanatory after you've visited: **http://bit.ly/exclusivepdfs.**

We hope you'll enjoy our free bonuses as much as we enjoyed preparing it for you!